THE NYAFF

SCOTTISH POEMS IN ENGLISH AND SCOTS

WINDFALL BOOKS

TOM HUBBARD

Dedicated to the memory of Duncan Glen 1933-2008

The right of Tom Hubbard to be identified as author of this work
has been asserted in accordance with the
Copyright, Designs and Patents Act 1988
A catalogue record for this book is available from the British Library

ISBN 978 0 9557264 5 3

Printed by Printing Services Scotland Ltd
Cover design by Claire Hubbard
Photography by Jamie Knight

Typesetting, layout and design by Windfall Books
Published by Windfall Books, Kelty
0044(0)1383 831076
windfallbooks@tiscali.co.uk
www.spanglefish.com/windfallbooks

2

ABOUT THE AUTHOR

TOM HUBBARD is a Fifer who was educated at Aberdeen and Strathclyde
Universities. He was the first Librarian of the Scottish Poetry Library, from
1984 to 1992, and went on to become an itinerant academic, though his
permanent home is in Kirkcaldy. In Fife Tom was Chairman of the Robert
Henryson Society (2002-05) and the first Chairman of the Fife Book Fair
Association (2009-11).
His previous poetry collections include: *Four Fife Poets* (with John Brewster,
William Hershaw and the late Harvey Holton; Aberdeen University Press),
Tak 5/Tak 50 (CD; with William Hershaw, Angus Martin, David C. Purdie
and David Purves; Scotsoun), *Scottish Faust:Poems and Ballads of Eldritch
Lore* (Kettillonia), *From Soda Fountain to Moonshine Mountain: American
Poems* (Akros), *Peacocks and Squirrels: Poems of Fife* (Akros), *The Chagall
Winnocks: wi ither Scots Ballants and Poems o Europe* (Book with CD;
Grace Note Publications). His novel, *Marie B.* (Ravenscraig Press), based on
the life of the Ukrainian painter Marie Bashkirtseff, was longlisted for a
Saltire book of the year award.

3

CONTENTS

1

2

3

4

1

FIFE CHILD IN THE FIFTIES

They've long demolished the side-street by the Links
That set me journeying when I was six or so:
In my grandmother's room I sensed the East –
Willow-pattern tea-chest, ottoman, divan, I know

As concepts now, mere concepts. Then, I gasped
At the elephant knick-knack carried from Ceylon
By her brother. From her window to the Forth
I saw Pacific islets, sunset deepening on

Silhouettes of palms. Later, I lifted the mask
To a scene of funeral pyre, volcanic pit:
The gong of a metal tub filled for my granddad
Black from the back-shift, coal-dust in his spit.

2001

AIBERDEEN ELEGIE-SCHERZANDO

*In affectiounate memorie o my PhD supervisor, Robin Gilmour 1943-
1999, eident scholar o the Victorian period*

There wis this Fifer loun came here ti byde,
And there wis a new Scots athin his lug:
His kintra yit, but o a different sooch
As his halflin nerves wad this and that wey rug
Wi the pynt and coonterpynt o growein up.
A city seemin harsk, but wi the grup
O kindlie hames that host, than lat ye gae
Whaur they've prepared ye: Embro, then Grenoble,
Connecticut, Budapest, Asheville NC,
Embro again; whit, man, can ye nou pree -
Govin frae a Royal Mile caff – the visible echoes
O Upperkirkgate, there at the North Brig?
Ye'll mynd thon first rare hairst o saxtie-nine,
The granite glisterin as the sun wad set,
Fit prologue ti yer unkent northren lichts,
The keenness in yer lugs, (forby yer loins)
Aiberdeen, Embro, grey stane ti the broun,
But their architectural pirlicues maist sib:
Thon's your Victorian studies, new applied
Frae whan you'd Robin Gilmour as your guide.

Say I'd been kidnapped in a fremmit airt,
Then drugged and bundled somehou back ti Scotland
And dumped blinfauldit in the Aist-Coast train
Atween twa touns a hunner mile apairt,
I'd 'ken masel' bi ilkane's 'queer-like smell'
The whilk wis Lang-Toun lino, or Footdee fush.
I mynd my airliest cless in Aiberdeen,
No i the lecture-haa, but the canteen,
Whan fair bumbazed bi the nouvelle cuisine:

6

Picter this speirin student frae Kirkcaddie,
And the kitchie-deem repones, 'At's skirlie, laddie!'

Honour ti aa wha steired a chiel's formatioun
In maitters great (and smaa) held in remembraunce,
Wi bygane period and present natioun
Alertin this young lad ti his resemblaunce
Ti fowk ayont himsel an's nairra gate.
Honour ti aa wha freed him frae the blate
And bummlin mainner guairdit wi a scowl,
As though he'd spun a haar attour his sowel;
Honour ti mentors wha cam unexpeckit –
Nae least the lassies wha his corp unsneckit.

The reuch refined music o Scots and Scotland
That's aye despised as faur as it's unkent:
I had a leid lost, efter my bairnheid,
My Fife speik o the playgrun silenced, sent
Ti a forgotten blur o embarrassment.
I tell the names, Robin, o your fellaeship
O ghaists whase sooch hushies doun College Boonds:
Dauvit Murison, wi his great leet o words
Matchin their historie's grandeur ti their soonds;
Matthew McDiarmid, and his serene wit
That merks the humane – in New King's he revealed
Cupar's, Dunfermline's makars; he unsealed
Oor tragic fables, wi voice and gesture fit.

And he, lately taen frae's, met years efter
In Embro's Tweeddale Coort: thon rare George Bruce,
Wha telt me, wi thon rocklike tender lauchter
O hou my letter lay sometime in's hoose
As he wunnered hou he'd fill a page or three
O Tam Hubbard's Mercat Press anthologie.
Then he speiks o crabs and clams – and the years atween

7

Twa students fade, ti the beach at Aiberdeen.
'I lowped frae my bed, ae nicht, like some gytit cratur,'
Says George, 'ti scrieve the lines o my conchologie,
Then sent you *Weys o Self-Preservin Natur.*'

Echo cries ti echo alang the Don Street waas
Veerin in and oot aa wrang ti rationalitie,
As frae a neuk or a pend some view fair strikes ye
Gin ye're a student at the stert or the end o yer fower-year:
Aiblins i the hairst, as Sanct Machar's touers rise sterk
At the yalla-cramasie lift, and ye've scarce taen in the glorie o't,
Fir you're ower young, yit – or aiblins i the simmer,
Ye've bevvied and sung and daunced neth the Northren Lichts –
Thon Aurora that augurs nocht but an unkent future.
Seaton Park trysts, the chimes: tak leave o't aa,
'The Dee, the Don, Balgounie Brig's bleck waa.'

Ya nye Baïron. – He's nae Byron, the chiel
Whase cup, and thus his kyte, fair runneth over;
Wha, at the hingin doun o's jowels, wad dover
Ower his abandoned hopes fir the Commonweill.
Up, man! Dinna cleik wi the times;
There wis keech, there wis sang, i the heid yince daurk and curly
Speirin at mair nor whit the hell wis skirlie:
Dinna scowk i the blandwagon rowlin ower social crimes.
A clessroom drained o umwhile eloquence
Can, i the myndin o't, mak recompense,
Tho deid and leevin mell i the great unseen.
Match twal-through-nineteenth centurie sensibilities
Ti twenty-first centurie debilities,
Adoptit prodigal son o Aiberdeen.

2002

THE HOOSE O LICHT

*Praise-poem ti Patrick Geddes and his successors in Embro's cultural
revival*

We biggit a land:
A mony-layered tenement,
And as it rose, we scarcely kent
That sic a shooglie pile wad stand
The blufferts o the north. We feared
Fir murlie waas wi the bleck rot,
The clock's quick chaps.
                                    But then appeared
The traivelled fowk wha socht a hame,
Wha lairned us even as we lairned thaim.
Mithers fund rest there wi their weans
And sang the lines we'd lang forgot;
We welcomed chiels wi metal and pent,
Ti limn their legends i the stanes;
Sae wi the turn o a shair hand
They wove a spiral frae the sand.

We riggit oor space,
That we cuid constellate the years
O the lang mirk and the tentit base
Wi the words o oor ain and the warld's seers;
This is oor ootleuk touer: a guide
Fir the passin pilgrims ower the tide.

2000

9

ST BERNARD'S WELL

Our duty is to free that water - Hugh MacDiarmid

Young they were when they found the source,
Guddling at the pebbles and leaping up the rock-
The fountain pappled, and the woodland chattered
While the town rose high, sedately, block by block.

Squares and circles and crescents,
Spires and monuments, ranks of iron fence
And lamp-posts, sentinels of silence
Decked in their verdigris, possess no force

Against these boys, exultant denizens
Claiming their castle here above the surge:
For there were dens and duns of Scotland past
Each with its rhythm, boldly to emerge

In all its raw refinement, to the sea.
May all our bairns draw up this mingled lore,
Steel-pointed charts for their discovery
Of the quickening shadows cast beyond our shore.

10

For those of us have sought new kin among
Oceanic exiles, Indian healers, the monochromatic
And multifaceted Baltic to Balkan bards
Whose gestures must continue enigmatic.

Richer demarcations between pure and impure
Channels destined to merge by cliffs and dunes:
Drink, and the devil may (or may not) ensure
We're free of internal cataracts, typhoons,

That the dank valleys yield us such a dram
Luminously through our mordant afternoons:
We prodigals, homefully travelling
To the snell temple over the hot spring.

2000

LEGEND O KING DAVIT AND THE STAG

King Davit o Scotland
Wandered by the Berwick strand.

The haar thickened ower the Firth;
The king threw 's sword inti the yirth.

Gulls focht craws wi bitter skreeks:
Bluid drapped frae their beaks.

A deid knicht kest upon the rock
Stared at the king as if ti mock:

His chaps moved as in speikin. 'Hail!
Sir king: whit gars ye look sae pale?

'Oor tribal hatreds winna cease;
Oor kintra never sall ken peace.

'Oor bairns at play sall dee in pain,
For this is Satan's prime domain.

'Nor piety nor poetry
Can challenge this oor destiny.'

King Davit o Scotland
Heard these words on Berwick strand,

And ever efter, in his dreams,
Socht the single act that redeems,

Redeems the failures o his reign
When bairns at play cuid dee in pain.

Thus Davit o Scotland socht ti choose
The wey o Davit, King o the Jews,

An umwhile sinner o gross exemple,
Wha abasit himsel and biggit a temple.

But thocht is thrall and words are braith,
Sae Scotland's Davit forgot his aith.

In Embro Castle he fairly rins
Throu each o the seiven deidly sins.

Sae ti his courtiers he'll can say
'I'll gang ti the hunt on the Sabbath day.'

His faither-confessor shaks his heid
As the king saddles his finest steed.

Upon the slopes o Arthur's Crag
Davit o Scotland pursues the stag -

But here's an unco kind o thing,
The stag turns roond and pursues the king!

'Mercy o God, sall I at last,
Bi a dumb baest be stekit fast?

'And by nae priest absolvít
Be shaken aff intil the pit,

Then sall Auld Nick lauch lood and say,
The hunt's brocht us braw meat the-day.'

The king reached oot agin his weird,
Cleikit the air, and grew mair feared:

Then, 'tween the antlers risin up,
A Haly Cross wis in his grup!

He wis hurled in a pile o leaves and sticks:
Vainished were stag and crucifix.

Thon nicht, a voice cried in his dreams
Fir the single act that redeems.

Sae on the morn King Davit begoud
Ti bigg the Kirk o the Haly Rood.

Ablow the slope o Arthur's Seat,
As ane o 's labourers, he maun sweit;

Fir wha grups the cross, maun grup the trowel,
Ti save his body forby his sowel.

Sae they raised thon kirk, that it suid be
Fir the common folk a sanctuarie.

And bairns unborn sall bless his reign,
That there they'll no cuid dee in pain.

This is the tale, forby the tune
O king Davit, thon 'sair sanct fir the croun'!

2004

14

SHARAKUEN

And we sall come again ti this yett
By the Stane o Walcome and the Stane o Bydin,
Ti an Eden o the East, within the West.

We sall ken it as it wis:
The mell o choice and chaunce,
The skeelie haund and the birkie hairt,

O the makar within his wark,
No made, but aye in makkin,
No afore or efter, but *nou*:

Athort the kinkin brig
Ti the tea-hoose on the inch:
'The freithy bree o jade.'

And we sall pairt at the shore,
Ane ti his aesomeness,
Yont cedar and cypress and sauchie,

Ti growe juist as they growe,
Withoot their ever ettlin:
Oor lairnin's a forgettin.

By the watter-lilies and lanterns,
By the deas that honours guests,
By the rock whaur the sea-gull rests,

Aa nou as it wis then,
Sained by the God o the Ben:
Sharakuen, sharakuen.

1991

15

2

VIGIL

The April of the great frost:
We were seized, tied, freeze-dried paper-thin
Like headlines blowing, *Come the morn, we'll win:*
Or lose, perhaps, with fingers double-crossed.

The daft auld limmer shivers on the hill:
She has nae flair, her bairns hae kest her oot;
Time wis, fowk said, 'We'll keep ye, hen, frae the chill.
We'll roast ye ti a bing o banes and soot!'

Aiblins the-day she's feart ti meet thae tykes
That huddle roun the burner endlessly:
'Come, mither, jyne us at the guairdit dykes:
They've locked the door and bunged awa the key.'

Her voice (the tykes said) wis nae carlin's speik:
A young-like lassie on the road, aamaist.
They watched her beauty vanish in the reek -
Wis she a wumman, thon, or else a ghaist?

The Saltire flies over St Andrew's House.
There's fireworks on MacDiarmid Boulevard.
Republic Day's a carnival carouse
As Scottish men try hard not to be hard.

'Course, it's a game, just. Harmless way to rest.
It makes a change from fitbaa, and that's good.
The Scottish Secretary's fair impressed;
It's doubtful, though, if he has understood.

When Czechs have sung 'Where is my home?'
We'll grunt 'No dosh? – No room at the inn!'
We'll sell the Euros a kilted gnome
With a pawky wee North-British grin.

He'll come complete with his but-and-ben
(A Scotsman's home is not his castle)
And his deferential vote, ye ken,
Eliminating any hassle.

What, flower of Scotland? Terrace-stuff!
Election night, we'll show who's boss.
Don't come it with that soulful guff:
Most of us couldn't give a toss.

Oor gnome's the ideal Embro guide:
At culture, too, he's most kenspeckle;
Although he looks like Mr Hyde,
He'd more than pass for Dr Jekyll.

Oor intelligentsia? Puir sowels,
Pontificatin through their bowels;
Postmodernism's pic ' n' mix
Is aa their intellectual kicks.

Scotland's cultural independence
Is clear to anyone who looks:
They've taen folks' cairdboard boxes awa,
Recycled thaim inti poetry buiks.

They've smothered sexuality
With jargon-friendly, fake polemics:
Intertextuality
Between consenting academics.

Aince makars sang it rare and roch –
Their darg wis clear, sans doobt,
No ti poure honey in the troch
But cowp the damn thing oot.

We're saved bi the *amadan naomh*, the holy fool;
La Mancha's on the Calton; Prof. Miguel
De Unamuno praised Don Quixote's rule –
Ti lowp wi faith abune the rational.

Travelling hopefully – biding to arrive –
You'll recognise a folk from where they've dossed.
How can a gangrel few remain alive?
They, who have not betrayed, have surely lost?

1992

TRUMPTY NUMPTY: ANE FLYTE

Trumpty Numpty sat on his buttocks
With his private army of full-trousered puddocks

Ready to pounce at just the right time
And cover the land with their ugsome slime

Trumpty Numpty shat on his hunkers
While the fearties kept mom and crept wide of the bunkers

Yup: Trumpty Numpty had it all
Till his toupée took an unfortunate fall

Right beside a cake of bovine sharn,
On this windy coast. Trumpt muttered, 'Darn,

Where's my goddam hairpiece? Is this it,
Or some Scattish hillbilly's cattle shit?'

And all Trumpty's army and all Trumpty's men
Couldnae put the right bodypart on him again

So oor Darnauld honours his mom indeed
With such Scottish soil upon his heid

And dontcha jest feel kinda sentimental
At a sight so inspiringly excremental?

See him a-wearin' this monstrous bap
Which'll serve just as well for his Doctor's cap

While a uni sinks in odorous odium
As himself waddles up in his gown to the podium
2010

THE CHOOB

or LA COMMEDIA GLASVEGIANA (SCOTTISH TYPES #1)

Whit's a subcrawl?
A choob in the choob.

There's fifteen staps on the subway,
　　But the choob, he disna care,
Tho he gets aff at ilka stap
　　And it's seeven pund – an mair –

Fifteen staps o the subway,
　　And the choob is on the loose:
He's voued that, ilka stap, he'll heid
　　Fir the nearest bevvy-hoose.

Fifteen staps o the subway –
　　Whit recks he o the fare?
Fifteen staps o the subway,
　　But no juist fifteen stair.

Aaready at Buchanan Street
He's gey unsteidy on his feet.

He decants at Coocaddens;
The media-folk's fly-patter maddens.

At Sanct George's Croce he fins relief,
Zips up, then, 'See's anither, chief',

Frae Kelvinbrig ti Hillheid
His faculties are Ph.Deid.

Haurd stares at Kelvinhaa and Partick:
He knocks thaim back, double(s)-quick,

But risks his neck at Govan and Ibrox,
Croonin at the baur and talkin bollox.

Cessnock and Kinnin Park,
Tryin ti keep doun the guid wark;

Shields Road and West Street,
There's an elephant in a kilt but naebody else can see't.

Brig Street and Sanct Enoch,
He guesses he's feelin kinda roch,

But a Scottish choob's no easy beat
Sae he sterts aa ower at Buchanan Street –

He's in his circle o the doomed –
Till the subway – and himsel – are toomed –

1991

THE NYAFF

(SCOTTISH TYPES #2)

Gin you wad ken the NYAFF, think on the word.
Ane nebstril heezed at you gin that you were
A duggie's tolie he had trodden on;
The N enters your lug, slaw, leesurely,
Tweestin, searin sherp and neat,
Then the YAAAAAA crescendos as ti brust your heid –
A siren warnin o invasioun –
Then, sudden, the FFff faas fortissimo,
His teeth upon his lip ti shut you oot.
O, but you'd grien ti enter wi your fist!
You yoursel pronounce the word quick eneuch –
NYAFF. A snotterie N, the Y a hint
o YOU, PISS (understuid), then AFF, git aff
o ma kintra! – YOU PRISS AFF, YE SLEEKIT NYAFF –
No that there's ever a nyaff at wisna sleekit
As we've kent syne seeventeen-seeven (at the least).

A Scottish type? O ay! He's shair he's Scottish:
It's awfly nyice to be beck in the mutha countri,
At a taïme like this. I'd retha live in Enbra
Than any utha citi in th Yoo Kay.
So many concets, opra, prahvate views,
Bk launches – Scotland's netional drink: chp waïne!
Chp waïne, indeed, the natives always waïning.
Nevah maïnd: I even knew the Gay Lick f Scotland,
And wen I pronyced it ELBA, I got the job.

ELBA indeed! Gin that he's sic a Scot,
You'd lang ti drap him on a faur-oot inch
A hunner mile due west o Papa Westray.
He's a dominator i the guise o a liberator,
He's the verra Nyaffoleon Bonyaffarte o nyaffs:
- Tho true, that's faur frae fair on the Empriour
Wha wisna near successfu as oor nyaff.

Tho rare wad be 's retrait frae Edinbro,
Snaw cuidna freeze him oot: he'd freeze the snaw.

1991

23

QUATRAINS FOR A NEW WORLD ORDER

i.m. Adrian Mitchell 1932-2008

1

Ye Banks and Buroos of bonny Boom
And Bust, of Boost and boney bum:
Come, whirl a gig upon our tomb.
Pray, weep for us: we were so dumb.

2

The Minister at the podium
Hands out vinegar lollipops,
Stops and stares,
Blethers on about shared values and even more (or less) valued shares.

3

Read *The Hampstead Review of Books*
In its Guardianly glory,
Assisting a tribal mother
In selling her son's sad story.

4

I mind of a New England factory:
Women thread-workers struck for equal pay;
While at the local university
Profs knitted arguments from day to day,

Thrusting themselves right up the tenure-track,
With Fair Trade jewelry dangling from their wrists.
Their sisters lost the fight and shuffled back,
Asking themselves: *Where were those Feminists?*

5

This is the new dialectic:
Being uptight in a downturn.
Carlyle was merely dyspeptic,
And Ruskin was nuts, we learn,

As was Blake. Who now reads Marx
On commodity fetish, eh?
Settle down. Be very afraid.
We've got your DNA.

6

Fascism's a fashion statement. Come, take my invisible hand,
For Auld Lang Europe's sake. Join Sarkolusconi's band.
Cover your arse in Britishness and fix some referendum:
You may exploit folk (by all means) but you must not offend them.

2008

3

ANCESTRAL VOICES

1

It was a village mashed into a suburb,
Served by a train that shook the tracks to groaning,
A plastic and metal, grimed and bubblegummed
Demented creeping insect, casting off folks;
Some young, most entering middle-middle age
- Like Leslie Wick, now slouching through the underpass.

Leslie taught maths back at the city college
That had a problem in renaming itself
In line with an image relevant to the times
And statistical fiddling by the government.
Les wasn't in decisions, and cared less,
But as a man who had some truck with numbers
He knew that an awful lot just didn't add up.

He recalled often the words of his late mum:
'Keep your ears open, son, and your mouth shut.'

Little these words had served his mum herself.
Young, she had heard words sweeter – and shyly nodded –
By a handsome uniform. Clicking of heels,
Kissing of hands – so Leszek, far from his country,
Charmed the local girls. She thought he'd never cheat her
Thought *she* was the lucky one – until he beat her.
Leszek Nowicki – name that made her sick –
And so she changed her son's to … Leslie Wick.

Through the estate he climbed, shaking his head,
Mumbling a phrase inaudible to himself;

Fumbling, as if he had forgotten something,
With the zip of the shopping bag he'd filled for one.
Up Kenilworth Terrace, crossing Ivanhoe Drive,
Stumbling on the road cut up for cable TV.

The original village, sure, was pretty enough:
Back at the staff canteen
They'd told him he was lucky living there,
Its traditional architecture, underrated;
What of these formulae upon the lintels,
The initials of each couple, with the date
Of their entry? *There's* an algebraic challenge
For lonely Les – 'Come on, pal, don't you see,'
His colleagues teased, 'that unlike us, you're free?'

2

The narrow vennels, through the centuries
Of families living there, twisted on and up,
Broke into steps and railings at their steepest
Where they met the ancient high street, lining the ridge.
A hill-top saw the village's beginnings,
Straddled with kirks and inns – a Scots community,
In equal measure holy and thirsty both.

A quiet place now, except for the young incomers.

At the west end of the high street, highest point
Of the ridge and of the village, its sometime centre.
The mercat square, the town house, and the courtroom,
Tower and steeple – a Protestant campanile –
And all long since unhaunted
By merchants, provosts, sheriffs and ministers.
Still, back a quarter-century or so,
People recalled that the complex's lower floor

Had housed a co-op – locally called 'the store'.

Now college property, it was divided
Into apartments, bedsits, for the students;
Zigzag of corridors on identical floors,
Their staunch intimidating hush offset
By livelier public spaces – here a games room,
There a cafeteria; and, as for culture,
Video projection room; more fitfully,
Guitar recitals, readings, in the basement
That even housed (though a decade or so ago)
A theatre, intimate and avant-garde.
Discos there now, or serious partying
That had the uneven stairs and vestibules
Criss-cross with lives who looked ahead to seize
Immortal marriages and mortgages.

But a quiet place, this village, spite of the incomers.

Incomers? An older one was Leslie Wick,
And few were quieter than our Les.
He had a set of rooms within the tower,
Poky, but adequate for a bachelor.
'I'll tell you this,' he'd say, 'it's a retreat.
High up, so I'm not bothered with the noise.
There's nobody in the block who's taught by me,
So I work long with minimal interruption.'
(His colleagues laughed.) 'I've got my telescope
And count the stars. I take the path through the forest,
Look up to the window of my little cell.
Life could be worse. No ties. I've my own ways,
Nobody changes them. I'm conscientious,
As you all know: I teach, and get results.'
His colleagues sighed. 'Leslie, it's just not fair.
You're well-defended from the void out there …'

Yet something ached in Leslie, and he knew it.
Not sex, precisely: deep in an equation,
He enjoyed orgiastic sublimation.
Perhaps some obstacle to his career,
Or growing older, and retirement nearer,
For what was Leslie Wick without his work?
Nobody knew the source of his distress.
What's certain was his fondness for the forest,
As if he heard an echo from the pines
Calling him on – as if for revelation
Of a tortuous mathematical solution.
He took the cobbled lane that sloped from the tower
Past the ruined kirk, and the small triangular graveyard
Whose narrowest point joined to the iron wicket,
Marking the border of village and wilderness.
Two worn steps down the gate, and the lane became track,
Muddy and nettled … Leslie still went on,
With a backward glance to the upper graveyard dyke,
And the stone, still firm and neat, of Mrs Wick:
The last grave ever dug on that narrow patch.
His mum had claimed the precious plot for herself!
They'd never move her. Never dare. But Les
Couldn't look there long. Enough that she remained,
Fixed on a line between his tower and the track.

On, on he went – Les and his solo walk,
Nodding his usual pleasure to the ferns;
For over the years he'd watched them curled and waiting,
Bearing their future quite unfussedly,
In sequence annual, repetitive, ancient.
Poised intricacies always comforted Les,
And as the ferns, so was the forest through,
So finely drawn against the gloaming sky;
The spiky lines criss-crossing, drawing him on,
As to a witch's kiss.

Suddenly Les
Thought he could hear what he'd never heard before –
A moaning sound – an animal caught in a trap?
Strangest of all (upon this windless night)
He couldn't figure out the source of the noise,
Both everywhere and nowhere, as it seemed.
And if he found it, what would he do next?
First aid to wildlife hadn't been on his syllabus.

A forest yields no answers: Leslie knew that,
As if by instinct. Memories of his father
Were limited and vague – though the desertion
Abrupt as it was, seemed natural to Les
Even as a child. Now, treading the leaf mould,
He called up the dark voice of Leszek Nowicki
Recounting folk tales to his little son,
Of mad old women lurching from village to village
And the wild bison thundering through the woods …

The moaning died away, as if to sleep.
Even Leslie felt he should get home to bed,
Though often before he'd gone on later and farther.
It was as if the sound had spoken to him,
In a sadly intimate tone,
That this wilderness was never his alone.

3

Men and women and contrivances,
Intersections of groups in elevators
And concourses at the exact moment required,
The same people in the same seats at the same hour:
A smooth unsmiling regiment pursuing
Chilled anarchies that click on different screens
With one insistent note. The relaxations

30

Of a similar pattern, yet there were exceptions.
One evening Les, as a senior resident,
Attended a reception in the tower
To welcome the new intake from abroad.
Awkward at first, the party livened up
When a soil scientist got slightly drunk
'Some day I will be President of my country' –
And a woman in a sari, come from a lab
Where she dissected rats, now hushed the guests
With her own verses, gnomic, spangled with images
From her inland province. Leslie found himself
The only Scotsman in the company.
A grinning moustache that bathed in orange juice
Held Les with a rich rhetoric on his nation,
Its oil, its plunderers both there and here;
This, with a wary glance across the room,
And a dropping of the voice, near Les's ear.

Les took it in, with the glasses of cheap wine,
And there was a haze in his hearing that caught
                              certain moments of clarity –
The fall of communism, the prospects for a social market,
Shopping malls patrolled by security firms,
The underclass of guest-workers in European cities.
At last through the verbal mesh, his eyes smarting
                              from a welter of competing tobaccos,
And near to fainting,
Leslie noticed the short, dumpy girl in the corner,
Who spoke little and had little spoken to her.
Half an hour before the party dispersed,
Les managed to ask her up to dance.
He liked her hint of a voice through the thudding rhythm,
Ended by kissing her cheek. She smiled, looked down.
Les heard his unbelieving inward niggle
That he'd never make a woman blush and giggle.

And she didn't. They'd meet in the cafeteria,
Les long-stirring the sugar in his cup,
Her eyelids heavy above a faraway frown.
You'd think them married and uncommunicative:
His colleagues winked – 'It's happened even to Les' –
But what had happened they could only guess.

She was Canadian, graduate in geology,
   That much was fairly known: but Les learned more –
     She was part Micmac, part Scots origin,
Would now and then allude to Indian lore
In a halting, homely manner. Awkwardly
     And earnestly she'd cast her wisdom in –
       To the most mundane of speech between these two:
     Les felt a mystery, and sought a clue.
       Little by little, every time they met,
         She'd make an utterance to him alone,
           Newly familiar, yet no less strange;
        Les heard her steady wordless undertone
       Invite, invoke. Whenever tête-à-tête
         Merges with pow-wow, two small lives must change.

    Yet Leslie's life had changed in such a way
At times it seemed more starkly what it was before.
    Unprecedented status of a boyfriend
Caused him to sense his hours of solitude the more.
    Where would it lead? He sought his forest paths –
     But they grew darker, he lost himself in brambles,
     Returned bleeding and confused.
                  When in the classroom
    He'd hear his voice as if it wasn't his own –
    The students' faces blurred, their whisperings
    Ominously irrelevant to maths.

Did Les and his Canadian
Now sleep together? Or, together, they slept?
At first,
To embrace was to embarrass. Once, to the sands
They took a bus-trip, and barely held hands.

At last - at last!
She being irked at their neighbours' and colleagues' mutterings,
The arch looks as at a pair of teenagers,
Fed up with edging apart when passing
                    certain groups of people or even buildings,
She pulled him towards her outside his door
'Come in, Leslie, I want to cuddle you' –
This small plain woman had transformed herself:
They jolted, as they fell, on Leslie's desk,
And the photo of his mum had to totter off,
Smash on the floor – as then and there,
Les uncontrollably precipitate,
Or the girl groaning late,
They clumsily consummated their affair.

Les limped moistly and in shock,
As the room grew darker with the girl's eyes
And she was the spirited daughter of the chiefs
Straining out of a weak man the stagnant chill of his beliefs.
Suddenly, she broke off. There was a quiver of light by the window,
As if the moon loomed strangely
                    through the branches of the single oak
In the hostel garden. She kissed her lover, ran from his room.
Les got up, washed, still dazed even as he knew he must follow her.
It was more than his own intent that led him from the tower,
Through the turns of the village and down the lane to the forest.
It grew darker but with tiny spasms breaking through,
Will-o-the-wisps dancing at the dark corner.
But then, as he felt he must swing the rusty gate of the graveyard,

33

The illuminations expanded to become swaying forms,
And he heard again the wail of the captive beast.
His lover was keening over the stones of her own people,
One half of that people, who centuries ago
Wept for their sons and daughters who crossed the ocean.
Leslie gripped a jutting edge of the graveyard wall:
His hand dripped blood as the dead approached
                              and arrayed themselves before him,
And he knew his mother was there, though her face
                              was either obscure or transparent.
Slowly from the phantoms came neither silence nor sound
But a pulse that accompanied the girl's lament-
If lament it was, and if Les was able to sense it
With ears and a body somewhere beyond his own.

The dead and the living raised palms towards the wilderness:
The man sought the woman, she sought him no less.
The spirits faded into the nightly forest hum;
Silent, unflurried, with one rare caress
Les held her waist. A last, waking welcome ...

1994 – 1995

34

4

RAVENSCRAIG ELEGY

For Duncan Glen

Cave and turret: silence with presence,
And an eldritch echo across the Forth.
Ten years since we walked to lunch at the Man in the Rock,
Discoursing of books and pamphlets: daftness and laughter.
There were labours past and to come,
Above Dysart harbour, which welcomes its children home.

Nature unknowingly saves for us her artefacts:
The stone seat by the path, the twisted tree
          where a girl plays with her dog,
So from the flux and flummox you rescued song.
The gull's cry and the wave's lap
          unmake to re-make themselves, as your long
Stravaiging halts, resumes and re-enacts.

2008

NOTES ON THE POEMS

p7 - *Cupar's, Dunfermline's makars*– respectively Sir David Lyndsay and Robert Henryson.

p8 - *Ya nye Baïron* – see the poems of Lermontov.

p15 - Sharakuen, which means 'a place of pleasure and delight' was the name of part of a Japanese garden near Dollar, Clackmannanshire, at the foot of the Ochil Hills; it was ravaged by weather and vandalism yet once there was a possibility of its restoration.

p16 - The 'vigil' was that for a Scottish Parliament. It was kept going until the 'Yes' vote in 1999. Part of the historical record only, or …?

p35 - Ravenscraig Park flanks the Fife shore between Kirkcaldy and Dysart, and is near the final home of Duncan Glen. He and his wife Margaret returned to Fife in 1996.

ACKNOWLEDGEMENTS

Some of these poems have previously appeared in the following publications: *Aberdeen University Review, Adrian: Scotland Celebrates Adrian Mitchell, Cothrom, Edinburgh: an Intimate City, Edinburgh Review, The Elphinstone Kist, Fox, Fras, Fringe of Gold, Lallans, Markings, Scottish Arts Council 'Poem of the Month' (May 2002), The Scottish Review* (ed. Kenneth Roy), *Spectrum, Under Cover.* I wish to express my thanks to their editors.

FURTHER NOTES ON THE AUTHOR

Tom Hubbard's non-fictional books include *Seeking Mr Hyde: Studies in Robert Louis Stevenson, Symbolism, and the Pre-Modern* (Peter Lang), *The Integrative Vision: Poetry and the Visual Arts in Baudelaire, Rilke, and MacDiarmid* (Akros) and *Michael Scot: Myth and Polymath* (Akros). He has edited or co-edited many other publications over the past three decades. In the spring semester of 2011 he was Lynn Wood Neag Distinguished Visiting Professor in the Department of English at the University of Connecticut, and subsequently Professeur invité, UFR des langues et lettres étrangères, Université Stendhal (Grenoble-3). During 2012 he was a Writer-in-Residence at the Château de Lavigny in Switzerland.